Quick Guide

Nora likes to play with her friends.

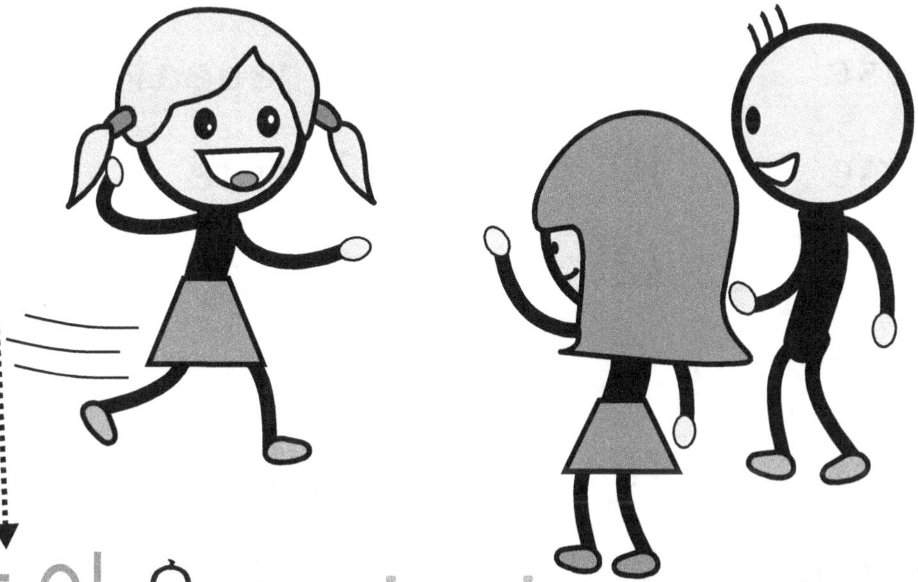

Korean → 놀아요 to play, hang out

no.ra.yo (nora + yo)

romanization

mnemonics (present tense)

pronounce the RED text **+ yo** or **hae.yo**

The mnemonics of this guide are in **PRESENT TENSE**.

Pronouns are rarely used in Korean. The other person can guess from context who you are referring to.
A verb conjugation for the verb 놀다 in the present tense:

- I play – 놀아요
- you play – 놀아요
- he plays – 놀아요
- she plays – 놀아요
- they play – 놀아요
- we play – 놀아요
- let's play – 놀아요

THE SAME

Korean Verbs

to buy
사다

<u>Sa</u>sha likes to buy things.

In Korean the **subject** (I/you/he/she/we/they) is often **left out**. 사요 sa.**yo** means to buy.
It can mean (I buy, you buy, she buys, he buys, we buy, they buy, let's buy, etc.)

Dictionary form: sa.da 사다
Present tense: 사요 sa.**yo**

to catch
잡다

잡아요 ja.ba.yo means to catch.
It can mean (I catch/you catch/she catches/we catch/they catch, etc.)

Dictionary form: 잡다 jap.da
Present tense: 잡아요 ja.ba.yo

to choose
사다

골라요 go.lla.yo means to choose, to pick. It can mean (I choose/you choose/she chooses/they choose/let's choose, etc.)

Dictionary form: 고르다 go.reu.da
Present tense: 골라요 go.lla.yo

to close

달다

달아요 da.da.yo means to close.
It can mean (I close/you close/he closes/we close
they close/let's close, etc.)

Dictionary form: 닫다 dat.da
Present tense: 달아요 da.da.yo

to come
오다

와요 wa.yo means to come.
It can mean (I come/you come/she comes/
they come, we come, etc.)

Dictionary form: oda 오다
Present tense   와요 wa.yo

to cut
자르다

잘라요 jal.la.yo means to cut.
It can mean (I cut/you cut/she cuts/they cut, etc.)

Dictionary form: 자르다 Ja.reu.da
Present tense: 잘라요 jal.la.yo

to do
하다

해요 hae.yo means to do.
It can mean (I do/you do/she does/we do/they do, let's do, do it, etc.)

Dictionary form: 하다 ha.da
Present tense: 해요 hae.yo

to drink
마시다

마셔요 ma.syeo.yo means to drink.
It can mean (I drink/you drink/she drinks/
they drink/let's drink, etc.)

Dictionary form: 마시다 ma.si.da
Present tense: 마셔요 ma.syeo.yo

17

to eat
먹다

먹어요 meo.geo.yo means to eat.
It can mean (I eat/you eat/she eats
we eat/they eat/let's eat, etc.)

Dictionary form: 먹다 meok.da
Present tense: 먹어요 meo.geo.yo

to fly
날다

날아요 nal.a.yo means to fly.
It can mean (I fly/you fly/he flies
we fly/they fly/let's fly, etc.)

Dictionary form: 날다 nal.da
Present tense: 날아요 nal.a.yo

to go
가다

가요 **ga**.**yo** means to go; to leave.
It can mean (I go/you go/she goes/we go,
let's go, etc.)

Dictionary form: 가다 ga.da
Present tense: 가요 ga.**yo**

to hate; dislike

싫다

실어요 si.reo.yo means to hate; to dislike.
It can mean (I hate/you hate/he hates
she hates/we hate/they hate, etc.)

Dictionary form: 싫다 sil.ta
Present tense: 실어요 si.reo.yo

to know
알다

알아요 a.ra.yo means to know.
It can mean (I know/you know/he knows
she knows/we know/they know, etc.)

Dictionary form: 알다 al.da
Present tense: 알아요 a.ra.yo

to live
살다

Mr. **Salami** lives with Miss Egg.

살아요 sa.ra.yo means to live.
It can mean (I live/you live/she lives/we live, etc.)

Dictionary form: 살다 sal.da
Present tense: 살아요 sa.ra.yo

to meet
만나다

man.na.yo 만나요 means to meet.
It can mean (I meet/you meet/she meets/
we meet, let's meet, etc.)

Dictionary form: man.na.da 만나다
Present tense: man.na.yo 만나요

to play
놀다

놀아요 No.ra.yo means to play, to hang out (with someone). It can mean (I play/you play/she plays/they play, we play, etc.)

Dictionary form: 놀다 Nol.da
Present tense: 놀아요 No.ra.yo

to pray
기도하다

기도해요 gi.do.hae.yo means to pray.
It can mean (I pray/you pray/he prays
we pray/they pray/let's pray, etc.)

Dictionary form: 기도하다 gi.do.ha.da
Present tense: 기도해요 gi.do.hae.yo

to read

읽다

읽어요 il.geo.yo means to read.
It can mean (I read/you read/she read/we read they read/let's read, etc.)

Dictionary form: 읽다 ik.dda
Present tense: 읽어요 il.geo.yo

to repeat

반복하다

반복해요 ban.bog.**hae.yo** means to repeat.
It can mean (I repeat/you repeat/he repeats we repeat/they repeat/let's repeat, etc.)

Dictionary form: 반복하다 ban.bok.ha.da
Present tense:　 반복해요 ban.bog.**hae.yo**

to ride
타다

타요 ta.yo means to ride.
It can mean (I ride/you ride/she rides/
he rides/they ride, let's ride, etc.)

Dictionary form: 타다 ta.da
Present tense: 타요 ta.yo

to sit

앉다

The baby likes to sit on Jack.

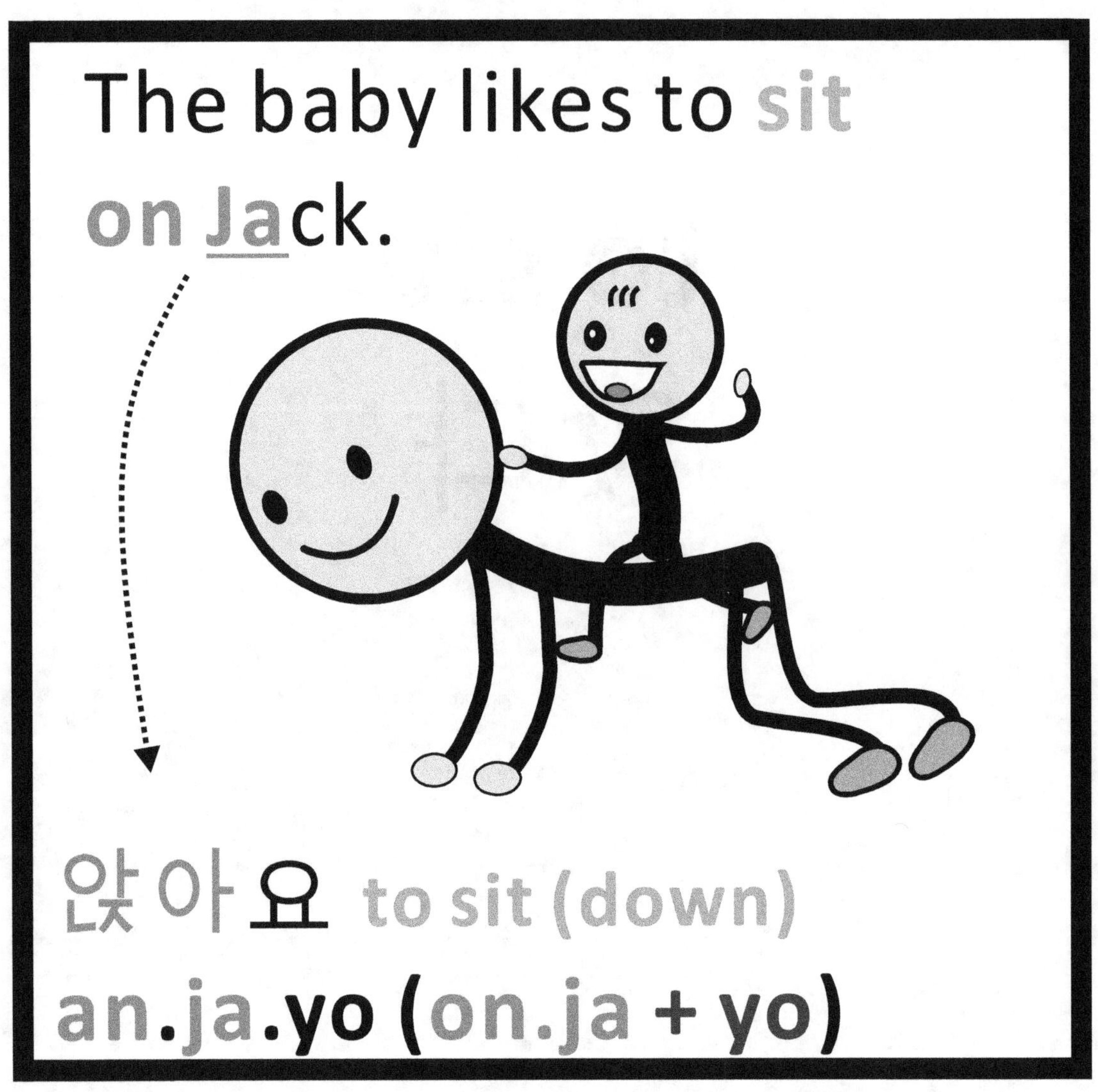

앉아요 to sit (down)

an.ja.yo (on.ja + yo)

앉아요 an.ja.**yo** means to sit. It can mean
(I sit/you sit/she sits/they sit, please sit, etc.)

Dictionary form: 앉다 an.da
Present tense: 앉아요 an.ja.yo

to sleep
자다

자요 ja.yo means to sleep. It can mean
(I sleep/you sleep/she sleeps, we sleep, they
sleep, let's sleep, etc.)

Dictionary form: 자다 ja.da
Present tense: 자요 ja.yo

to stop; prevent
막다

막아요 mag.a.yo means to stop, to prevent
It can mean (I stop/you stop/he stops
they stop/let's stop, etc.)

Dictionary form: 막다 mak.da
Present tense: 막아요 mag.a.yo

to study
공부하다

공부해요 gong.bu.**hey.yo** means to study
It can mean (I study/you study/she studies/we study/let's study, etc.)

Dictionary form: 공부하다 gong.bu.hada
Present tense: 공부해요 gong.bu.**hey.yo**

to be cold

춥다

추워요 chu.wo.yo means to be cold.
It can mean (I'm cold/you're cold/she's cold, etc.)

Dictionary form: 춥다 chup.da
Present tense: 추워요 chu.wo.yo

to be hot
덥다

더워요 deo.wo.yo means to be hot, to feel hot
It can mean (I'm hot/you're hot/he's hot
we are hot/they're hot/it's hot, etc.)

Dictionary form: 덥다 deop.da
Present tense: 더워요 deo.wo.yo

to be expensive
비싸다

비싸요 pi.sa.yo means to be expensive

Dictionary form: 비싸다 pi.sa.da
Present tense:　 비싸요 pi.sa.yo

to touch
만지다

만져요 man.jyeo.yo means to touch
It can mean (I touch/you touch/he touches
we touch/they touch, etc.)

Dictionary form: 만지다 man.ji.da
Present tense: 만져요 man.jyeo.yo

to wash/shower
씻다

씻어요 ssi.seo.**yo** means to wash; to shower.
It can mean (I wash/you wash/she washes, we wash, they wash, etc.)

Dictionary form: 씻다 **ssit.da**
Present tense: 씻어요 **ssi.seo.yo**

to work
일하다

일해요 il.**hey.yo** means to work.
It can mean (I work/you work/she works, we work they work, let's work, etc.)

Dictionary form: 일하다 il.**ha.da**
Present tense: 일해요 il.**hey.yo**

How to Conjugate Korean Verbs?
Present Tense (polite form)

Verbs in a Koran dictionary are in this form:

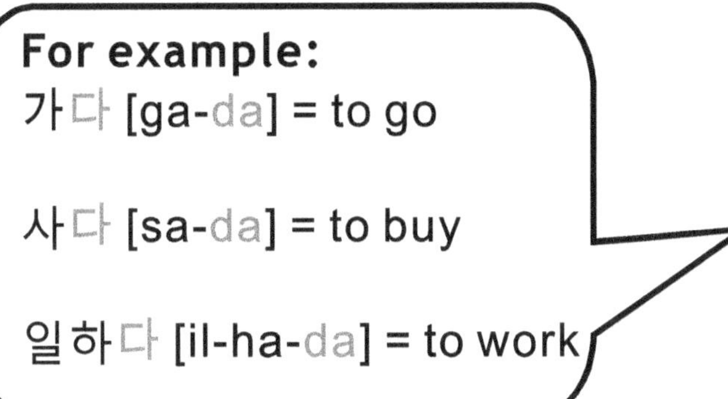

How to change from dictionary form into present tense form?
2 EASY STEPS:

STEP 1: Drop the last letter, 다 [da]. 가다 [ga-da] = 가 [ga]

STEP 2: Then ADD one of the following endings.

(a) 아요 [a-yo]   **(b)** 어요 [eo-yo]   **(c)** 여요 [yeo-yo]

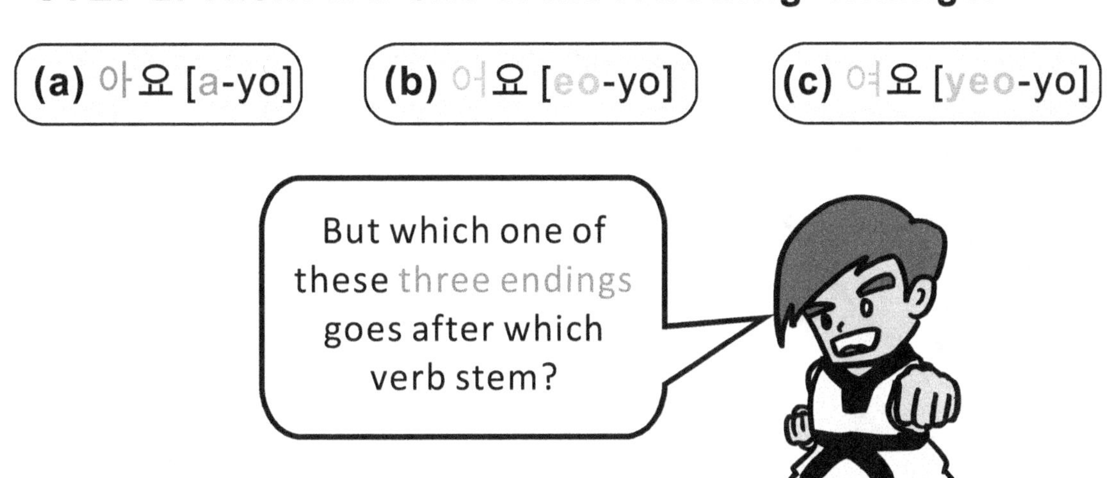

Please follow these guidelines!

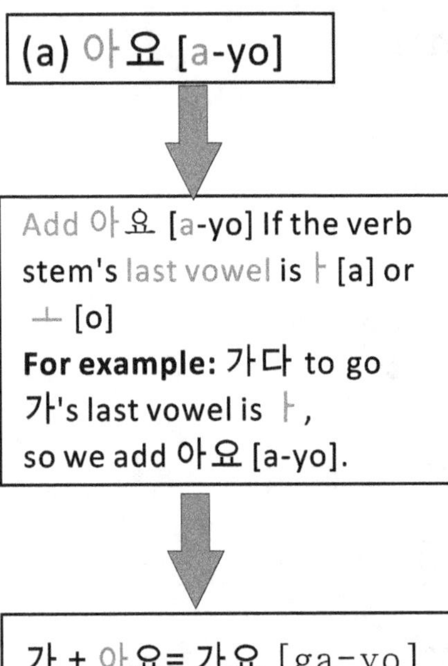

(a) 아요 [a-yo]

Add 아요 [a-yo] If the verb stem's last vowel is ㅏ [a] or ㅗ [o]

For example: 가다 to go
가's last vowel is ㅏ,
so we add 아요 [a-yo].

가 + 아요= 가요 [ga-yo]

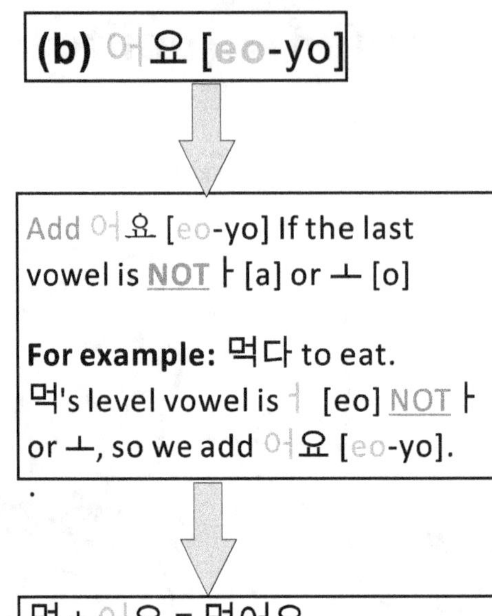

(b) 어요 [eo-yo]

Add 어요 [eo-yo] If the last vowel is **NOT** ㅏ [a] or ㅗ [o]

For example: 먹다 to eat.
먹's level vowel is ㅓ [eo] NOT ㅏ
or ㅗ, so we add 어요 [eo-yo].
.

먹 + 어요 = 먹어요
[meo-geo-yo]

(c) 여요 [yeo-yo]

Over time, 하+여요 became 해요

Change to 해요 [hae-yo] if the verb stem is 하[ha]

For example: 일하다 to work.
Verb stem is 하 [ha], so we change 하 to 해요

일하 + 해요= 일해요
(il-hae-yo)